EMMANUEL JOSEPH

EcoThreads, Smart Fashion for a Sustainable Future

Copyright © 2025 by Emmanuel Joseph

All rights reserved. No part of this publication may be reproduced, stored or transmitted in any form or by any means, electronic, mechanical, photocopying, recording, scanning, or otherwise without written permission from the publisher. It is illegal to copy this book, post it to a website, or distribute it by any other means without permission.

First edition

This book was professionally typeset on Reedsy. Find out more at reedsy.com

Contents

1. Chapter 1: The Birth of EcoThreads — 1
2. Chapter 2: The Environmental Impact of Fast Fashion — 3
3. Chapter 3: Understanding Sustainable Fashion — 5
4. Chapter 4: Innovative Materials and Technologies — 7
5. Chapter 5: The Role of Consumers in Sustainable Fashion — 9
6. Chapter 6: The Power of Ethical Fashion Brands — 11
7. Chapter 7: Traditional Techniques and Modern Innovations — 13
8. Chapter 8: Fashion and Circular Economy — 15
9. Chapter 9: The Role of Policy and Legislation — 17
10. Chapter 10: Education and Awareness — 19
11. Chapter 11: The Business of Sustainable Fashion — 21
12. Chapter 12: The Intersection of Fashion and Technology — 23
13. Chapter 13: The Future of Sustainable Fashion — 25
14. Chapter 14: Personal Journeys in Sustainable Fashion — 27
15. Chapter 15: A Call to Action — 29

1

Chapter 1: The Birth of EcoThreads

In the vibrant city of Lagos, Nigeria, where the bustling markets and vibrant colors weave a tapestry of culture and tradition, Aisha Adeyemi, a visionary fashion designer, began her journey. As a child, she watched her mother and grandmother handcraft beautiful textiles from locally sourced materials, instilling in her a deep appreciation for sustainable fashion. Growing up, Aisha was determined to revolutionize the fashion industry by combining her cultural heritage with modern technology. Her dream was to create EcoThreads, a fashion brand that would not only produce stylish and innovative clothing but also prioritize environmental sustainability.

In her early twenties, Aisha attended a prestigious fashion institute in Paris. There, she met Lucas, a brilliant tech enthusiast from Brazil who shared her passion for sustainability. They quickly became friends, and their shared vision of a greener fashion industry blossomed into a partnership. Together, they began researching and developing innovative materials and techniques that would reduce the environmental impact of clothing production.

One of their most significant breakthroughs came when they discovered a way to create fabric from recycled plastic bottles. This material, called EcoFiber, was not only durable and versatile but also environmentally friendly. With the help of Lucas's technological expertise, they were able to integrate smart textiles into their designs, creating garments that could monitor the wearer's health and adjust to temperature changes.

Their journey was not without challenges. They faced skepticism from industry experts who doubted the viability of their eco-friendly materials and designs. However, Aisha and Lucas persevered, fueled by their passion and determination. They traveled the world, visiting remote villages to learn traditional textile-making techniques and collaborating with local artisans to incorporate these methods into their designs.

EcoThreads quickly gained recognition for its innovative approach to fashion, and soon, their creations were featured on runways and in high-end boutiques. As their brand grew, Aisha and Lucas remained committed to their core values of sustainability and social responsibility. They established fair-trade partnerships with artisans and farmers, ensuring that everyone involved in the production process received fair wages and worked in safe conditions.

The success of EcoThreads inspired other designers and companies to adopt more sustainable practices, sparking a global movement towards eco-friendly fashion. Aisha's dream of revolutionizing the industry was becoming a reality, and her story continues to inspire future generations to pursue their passions while making a positive impact on the world.

2

Chapter 2: The Environmental Impact of Fast Fashion

The rise of fast fashion transformed the global fashion industry, making trendy clothing affordable and accessible to the masses. However, this convenience came at a significant environmental cost. The relentless pursuit of cheap, disposable fashion led to a surge in pollution, waste, and exploitation of natural resources.

Fast fashion's environmental impact is staggering. The production of synthetic fibers, such as polyester, relies heavily on fossil fuels, contributing to greenhouse gas emissions. Additionally, the textile dyeing process is one of the largest sources of water pollution globally, contaminating rivers and oceans with harmful chemicals. The industry generates massive amounts of textile waste, with millions of tons of clothing ending up in landfills each year.

Beyond the environmental consequences, fast fashion has severe social and economic impacts on local communities. Many garment workers, particularly in developing countries, endure exploitative working conditions, long hours, and low wages. The drive for ever-lower production costs often leads to unsafe work environments, as evidenced by tragic incidents like the Rana Plaza collapse in Bangladesh.

The relentless cycle of production and consumption in fast fashion has also led to a culture of disposability. Consumers are encouraged to buy more, wear items briefly, and discard them, fueling a never-ending demand for new clothing. This cycle perpetuates environmental degradation and social inequality, highlighting the urgent need for a more sustainable approach to fashion.

Despite these challenges, there is hope. Awareness of the environmental and social impact of fast fashion is growing, leading to increased demand for sustainable alternatives. Brands like EcoThreads are at the forefront of this movement, demonstrating that it is possible to create stylish, high-quality clothing while prioritizing sustainability and ethical practices.

3

Chapter 3: Understanding Sustainable Fashion

Sustainable fashion encompasses a holistic approach to clothing production and consumption, prioritizing environmental, social, and economic sustainability. At its core, sustainable fashion aims to minimize the negative impact of the fashion industry on the planet and people while promoting positive change.

One of the key principles of sustainable fashion is the use of eco-friendly materials. This includes organic fibers, such as cotton and hemp, grown without harmful pesticides and chemicals. Additionally, recycled materials, like EcoFiber, help reduce waste and conserve resources. Sustainable fashion also emphasizes the importance of ethical production practices, ensuring fair wages and safe working conditions for garment workers.

Several influential figures and organizations have played a crucial role in advancing the sustainable fashion movement. Designers like Stella McCartney and brands like Patagonia have championed eco-friendly materials and ethical practices, inspiring others to follow suit. Non-profit organizations, such as Fashion Revolution, advocate for greater transparency and accountability in the fashion industry, encouraging consumers to ask, "Who made my clothes?"

Despite the progress made, challenges remain in the sustainable fashion industry. Achieving true sustainability requires a collective effort from designers, manufacturers, consumers, and policymakers. Additionally, sustainable fashion often comes with a higher price tag, making it less accessible to some consumers. However, as awareness and demand for sustainable options grow, the industry continues to evolve and innovate.

The future of sustainable fashion holds great promise. With advancements in technology and materials, the possibilities for creating eco-friendly, stylish clothing are endless. By embracing sustainability, the fashion industry can pave the way for a more ethical and environmentally conscious future.

4

Chapter 4: Innovative Materials and Technologies

The development of innovative materials and technologies is at the heart of the sustainable fashion movement. These advancements are transforming the way clothing is produced, making it possible to create eco-friendly garments without sacrificing style or functionality.

Eco-friendly materials, such as organic cotton, hemp, and bamboo, have gained popularity for their minimal environmental impact. Organic cotton, for example, is grown without synthetic pesticides and fertilizers, reducing water consumption and soil degradation. Hemp, a highly versatile and durable fiber, requires minimal water and no pesticides, making it an ideal sustainable material. Bamboo, known for its rapid growth and biodegradability, is another excellent option for eco-friendly textiles.

Recycled materials, like EcoFiber, play a crucial role in reducing waste and conserving resources. By transforming plastic bottles and other waste products into fabric, EcoFiber helps divert waste from landfills and oceans. This innovative material is not only environmentally friendly but also durable and versatile, making it suitable for a wide range of clothing and accessories.

Technology is also revolutionizing sustainable fashion. Smart textiles, for instance, integrate electronic components into fabric, allowing garments to monitor the wearer's health, adjust to temperature changes, and even charge electronic devices. 3D printing is another groundbreaking technology, enabling designers to create intricate and customized garments with minimal waste. These technological advancements open up new possibilities for sustainable fashion, offering innovative solutions to traditional production methods.

Researchers and inventors are continually pushing the boundaries of sustainable materials and technologies. For example, scientists are developing biodegradable fabrics made from algae and other renewable resources. These materials not only reduce waste but also have the potential to sequester carbon, contributing to climate change mitigation.

The potential future advancements in sustainable fashion technology are limitless. As the industry continues to innovate and evolve, the possibilities for creating eco-friendly, stylish clothing are endless. By embracing these advancements, the fashion industry can pave the way for a more sustainable and ethical future.

5

Chapter 5: The Role of Consumers in Sustainable Fashion

Consumers play a crucial role in driving the sustainable fashion movement. By making conscious choices and supporting eco-friendly brands, individuals can significantly impact the fashion industry's environmental and social footprint.

Consumer awareness and education are essential in promoting sustainable fashion. Many people are unaware of the environmental and social consequences of their clothing choices. By educating themselves and others about sustainable fashion, consumers can make more informed decisions and advocate for change within the industry.

Individual choices can have a significant impact on the environment and the fashion industry. Simple actions, such as buying second-hand clothing, upcycling old garments, and supporting ethical brands, can help reduce waste and conserve resources. Additionally, adopting a "less is more" mindset and investing in high-quality, durable pieces can minimize the environmental impact of one's wardrobe.

Personal stories of consumers who have embraced sustainable fashion can inspire others to follow suit. For example, Emily, a university student from London, decided to overhaul her wardrobe after learning about the negative impact of fast fashion. She began shopping at thrift stores, upcycling old clothes, and supporting ethical brands. Her journey not only reduced her environmental footprint but also sparked a passion for sustainable fashion, leading her to start a blog to share her experiences and inspire others.

Social media and influencers also play a significant role in promoting sustainable fashion. Influential figures, such as bloggers and celebrities, can raise awareness about the importance of sustainability and showcase eco-friendly fashion choices. By leveraging their platforms, they can encourage their followers to make more conscious decisions and support ethical brands.

The collective efforts of consumers, combined with the growing demand for sustainable options, can drive significant change within the fashion industry. By making informed choices and advocating for sustainability, individuals can contribute to a greener and more ethical future for fashion.

6

Chapter 6: The Power of Ethical Fashion Brands

Ethical fashion brands play a crucial role in promoting sustainability and social responsibility within the fashion industry. These brands prioritize ethical practices, from sourcing materials to production processes, ensuring that their impact on the environment and society is positive.

One of the most inspiring success stories in ethical fashion is that of People Tree, a pioneering brand founded by Safia Minney. People Tree has been at the forefront of the fair-trade fashion movement, working with artisans and farmers in developing countries to create beautiful, handmade clothing. The brand's commitment to fair wages, safe working conditions, and sustainable materials has set a high standard for the industry.

Ethical fashion brands often face significant challenges, such as higher production costs and limited resources. However, their dedication to sustainability and ethical practices drives them to overcome these obstacles. For example, Veja, a French sneaker brand, has gained worldwide recognition for its eco-friendly footwear made from organic cotton, wild rubber, and recycled materials. Despite the challenges, Veja has remained committed to transparency and ethical production, proving that sustainability and success can go hand in hand.

These brands' stories highlight the impact of ethical fashion on local communities and the environment. By supporting fair-trade practices and sustainable materials, ethical brands contribute to economic development and environmental conservation. Their success also inspires other designers and companies to adopt more sustainable practices, further driving the movement towards a greener fashion industry.

For consumers looking to support ethical fashion brands, there are several ways to identify and choose responsibly. Researching a brand's values, sourcing practices, and production methods can provide valuable insights into its commitment to sustainability. Additionally, certifications such as Fair Trade, Global Organic Textile Standard (GOTS), and B Corp can help consumers make informed decisions.

The power of ethical fashion brands lies not only in their products but also in their ability to inspire change. By prioritizing sustainability and social responsibility, these brands set an example for the industry and encourage consumers to make more conscious choices.

7

Chapter 7: Traditional Techniques and Modern Innovations

Traditional textile-making techniques have been passed down through generations, preserving cultural heritage and craftsmanship. These techniques often emphasize sustainable practices, such as using natural dyes and hand-weaving fabrics, which have a minimal environmental impact.

In India, the art of block printing has been practiced for centuries. Artisans use hand-carved wooden blocks to print intricate designs on fabric, creating unique and beautiful textiles. This traditional method relies on natural dyes and sustainable materials, making it an eco-friendly alternative to mass-produced fabrics. Brands like EcoThreads collaborate with these artisans, incorporating block-printed fabrics into their collections and supporting local communities.

Similarly, in Guatemala, the art of backstrap weaving has been an essential part of Mayan culture for generations. Women use a simple loom, anchored around their waist, to weave intricate patterns and designs. This technique requires minimal resources and produces stunning, high-quality textiles. By partnering with Mayan weavers, EcoThreads celebrates and preserves this rich cultural heritage while promoting sustainable fashion.

Modern innovations in sustainable fashion often complement traditional techniques, enhancing their environmental benefits. For example, digital printing technology allows designers to create intricate patterns with minimal waste and water usage. By combining traditional craftsmanship with cutting-edge technology, sustainable fashion brands can create unique, eco-friendly garments that honor cultural heritage and reduce environmental impact.

The fusion of traditional techniques and modern innovations offers exciting possibilities for sustainable fashion. By embracing the best of both worlds, designers can create stylish, high-quality clothing that respects the environment and supports local communities.

8

Chapter 8: Fashion and Circular Economy

A circular economy is a regenerative system that aims to minimize waste and make the most of resources by keeping products and materials in use for as long as possible. In the context of fashion, a circular economy involves designing garments for longevity, encouraging recycling and upcycling, and promoting sustainable consumption practices.

The benefits of a circular fashion system are manifold. By reducing waste and conserving resources, a circular economy can significantly decrease the environmental impact of the fashion industry. Additionally, it can create economic opportunities by fostering new business models, such as clothing rental, repair services, and resale platforms.

Several brands and initiatives are embracing circular fashion, demonstrating its potential to transform the industry. For example, Eileen Fisher, a pioneering sustainable fashion brand, has implemented a take-back program that encourages customers to return their used garments. These items are then repaired, redesigned, or recycled, keeping them out of landfills and extending their life cycle.

Personal stories of individuals contributing to a circular fashion system can inspire others to adopt more sustainable practices. For instance, Sarah, a fashion enthusiast from New York, decided to embrace a minimalist wardrobe and invest in high-quality, timeless pieces. She also began upcycling old garments and organizing clothing swaps with friends, reducing waste and promoting sustainable consumption.

The future of circular fashion holds great promise. As more brands and consumers embrace the principles of a circular economy, the fashion industry can move towards a more sustainable and environmentally conscious future. By rethinking the way we design, produce, and consume clothing, we can create a fashion system that benefits both people and the planet.

9

Chapter 9: The Role of Policy and Legislation

Government policies and regulations play a crucial role in promoting sustainable fashion. By establishing standards and incentives for sustainable practices, policymakers can drive positive change within the industry and encourage businesses to adopt more eco-friendly practices.

Several existing policies have had a significant impact on the fashion industry. For example, the European Union's Waste Framework Directive sets targets for reducing textile waste and promoting recycling and reuse. Similarly, the UK Modern Slavery Act requires companies to disclose their efforts to prevent forced labor and human trafficking in their supply chains, encouraging greater transparency and accountability.

Activists and organizations advocating for policy change are essential in driving progress. Fashion Revolution, a global movement advocating for greater transparency and sustainability in the fashion industry, has been instrumental in raising awareness and pushing for legislative change. Their annual Fashion Revolution Week encourages consumers to ask brands, "Who made my clothes?" and demand greater accountability.

Implementing sustainable fashion policies comes with challenges and opportunities. Policymakers must balance the need for environmental protection with economic considerations, ensuring that regulations do not unduly burden businesses. However, well-designed policies can create a level playing field, encouraging innovation and investment in sustainable practices.

Individuals can also get involved in policy advocacy by supporting organizations that champion sustainable fashion and engaging with their local representatives. By raising their voices and demanding change, consumers can contribute to the development of policies that promote a greener and more ethical fashion industry.

The role of policy and legislation in sustainable fashion is crucial. By establishing clear standards and incentives, policymakers can drive positive change and create a more sustainable future for the fashion industry.

10

Chapter 10: Education and Awareness

Education and awareness are vital in promoting sustainable fashion and empowering individuals to make informed choices. By understanding the environmental and social impact of their clothing choices, consumers can contribute to a more sustainable fashion industry.

Several programs and initiatives aim to educate future designers and consumers about sustainable fashion. Fashion schools and institutions are increasingly incorporating sustainability into their curricula, teaching students about eco-friendly materials, ethical production practices, and the importance of social responsibility. For example, the London College of Fashion offers courses and workshops on sustainable fashion, equipping the next generation of designers with the knowledge and skills to create a more sustainable industry.

Personal stories of educators and students making a difference can inspire others to join the movement. For instance, Emma, a fashion design student from Milan, was inspired by a guest lecture on sustainable fashion. She decided to focus her final project on creating a collection made entirely from recycled materials, raising awareness among her peers about the importance of sustainability.

Fashion schools and institutions play a crucial role in fostering sustainability within the industry. By prioritizing education and awareness, they can equip future designers with the knowledge and skills to create eco-friendly and ethical fashion. Additionally, industry partnerships and collaborations can provide students with hands-on experience and real-world insights into sustainable fashion practices.

Individuals can also educate themselves and others about sustainable fashion through various resources, such as books, documentaries, and online courses. By staying informed and sharing their knowledge, they can contribute to raising awareness and promoting positive change within the industry.

The importance of education and awareness in sustainable fashion cannot be overstated. By empowering individuals with knowledge and encouraging informed choices, we can create a more sustainable and ethical fashion industry.

11

Chapter 11: The Business of Sustainable Fashion

The business of sustainable fashion is complex, involving a delicate balance of innovation, creativity, and ethical practices. While the journey can be challenging, it is also filled with opportunities for those who are passionate about creating positive change.

Market trends indicate a growing demand for sustainable fashion, driven by increasing consumer awareness and concern for the environment. Brands that prioritize sustainability can tap into this demand and build a loyal customer base. Additionally, sustainable fashion often commands higher price points, reflecting the quality and ethical practices behind the products.

Entrepreneurs in the sustainable fashion industry face unique challenges, such as sourcing eco-friendly materials, maintaining ethical supply chains, and managing higher production costs. However, these challenges can be overcome with creativity and innovation. For example, brands like Patagonia and Everlane have successfully navigated these hurdles by being transparent about their practices and building strong relationships with suppliers.

Innovation and creativity are key drivers of success in sustainable fashion. By experimenting with new materials, designs, and business models, entrepreneurs can differentiate themselves in a competitive market. For example, Reformation, a Los Angeles-based brand, has gained popularity for its stylish, eco-friendly clothing and commitment to transparency. Their success demonstrates that sustainability and style can go hand in hand.

For aspiring sustainable fashion entrepreneurs, it is essential to stay informed about industry trends and developments. Networking with like-minded individuals, attending industry events, and participating in sustainability-focused workshops can provide valuable insights and inspiration. Additionally, leveraging digital platforms and social media can help build brand awareness and connect with consumers who share similar values.

The business of sustainable fashion is evolving rapidly, offering exciting opportunities for those who are committed to making a difference. By embracing innovation, creativity, and ethical practices, entrepreneurs can create successful, sustainable fashion brands that resonate with consumers and contribute to a greener future.

12

Chapter 12: The Intersection of Fashion and Technology

The intersection of fashion and technology is revolutionizing the industry, offering new possibilities for sustainability and innovation. From wearable tech to artificial intelligence, technological advancements are transforming the way clothing is designed, produced, and consumed.

Wearable tech integrates electronic components into clothing, providing functionalities beyond traditional garments. For example, smart textiles can monitor the wearer's health, adjust to temperature changes, and even charge electronic devices. These innovations enhance the functionality and sustainability of clothing, offering exciting possibilities for the future of fashion.

Artificial intelligence (AI) is also making a significant impact on the fashion industry. AI-powered tools can analyze consumer preferences, predict trends, and optimize supply chains, reducing waste and improving efficiency. Additionally, AI can assist designers in creating customized garments, enhancing the creative process and reducing the environmental impact of mass production.

Blockchain technology is another groundbreaking innovation in sustainable fashion. By providing a transparent and secure way to track the supply chain, blockchain can ensure the authenticity and ethical sourcing of materials. This technology enhances transparency and accountability, allowing consumers to make informed choices and support ethical brands.

The potential impact of emerging technologies on sustainability is vast. By integrating technology into fashion, the industry can develop innovative solutions to traditional challenges, such as waste reduction, resource conservation, and ethical production. These advancements offer exciting opportunities for creating a more sustainable and efficient fashion industry.

However, the integration of technology into fashion also raises ethical considerations. Issues such as data privacy, labor rights, and environmental impact must be carefully addressed to ensure that technological advancements contribute to sustainability and social responsibility.

The intersection of fashion and technology holds immense potential for transforming the industry. By embracing these advancements, designers and brands can create innovative, eco-friendly garments that meet the needs of modern consumers while promoting sustainability.

13

Chapter 13: The Future of Sustainable Fashion

The future of sustainable fashion is filled with promise and potential. As awareness and demand for eco-friendly and ethical clothing continue to grow, the industry is evolving to meet these needs. Current trends and future predictions indicate a shift towards greater sustainability, innovation, and collaboration.

One of the key trends in sustainable fashion is the rise of circular economy practices. As more brands adopt circular models, the fashion industry is moving towards reducing waste and conserving resources. Innovations in recycling, upcycling, and biodegradable materials are driving this shift, offering new possibilities for sustainable fashion.

Visionary designers and brands are leading the way in sustainable fashion, pushing the boundaries of creativity and innovation. For example, Stella McCartney, a pioneer in eco-friendly luxury fashion, continues to explore new materials and techniques to minimize environmental impact. Her commitment to sustainability serves as an inspiration for the industry, encouraging others to follow suit.

Global events, such as climate change, are also influencing the future of sustainable fashion. As the urgency to address environmental challenges grows, the fashion industry is being called upon to play a more significant role in mitigating its impact. This shift is driving greater collaboration between designers, brands, policymakers, and consumers to create a more sustainable future.

The role of collaboration and innovation in shaping the future of sustainable fashion cannot be overstated. By working together and sharing knowledge, the industry can develop new solutions and drive positive change. Initiatives such as the Sustainable Apparel Coalition and the Fashion Pact demonstrate the power of collective action in promoting sustainability.

For individuals looking to stay informed and involved in the sustainable fashion movement, there are several ways to get engaged. Following industry news, participating in events and workshops, and supporting ethical brands are all valuable ways to contribute to the movement. By staying informed and advocating for change, consumers can play a crucial role in shaping the future of sustainable fashion.

The future of sustainable fashion is bright, offering exciting opportunities for innovation, creativity, and collaboration. By embracing sustainability and working together, the industry can create a positive and lasting impact on the planet and society.

14

Chapter 14: Personal Journeys in Sustainable Fashion

Personal journeys in sustainable fashion highlight the challenges and triumphs individuals face as they embrace eco-friendly and ethical clothing choices. These stories serve as powerful examples of the impact that individual actions can have on the environment and communities.

One such story is that of Daniel, a fashion designer from Berlin. After learning about the environmental impact of the fashion industry, Daniel decided to transform his brand into a sustainable fashion label. He faced numerous challenges, including sourcing eco-friendly materials and finding ethical suppliers. However, his determination and passion for sustainability drove him to overcome these obstacles. Today, his brand is known for its innovative designs and commitment to ethical practices, inspiring others to follow in his footsteps.

Another inspiring journey is that of Leah, a consumer from Toronto. Motivated by her concern for the environment, Leah decided to overhaul her wardrobe and embrace sustainable fashion. She began shopping at thrift stores, supporting ethical brands, and upcycling old garments. Her journey not only reduced her environmental footprint but also sparked a passion for sustainable living. Leah now runs workshops and shares her experiences on social media, encouraging others to make more conscious fashion choices.

The impact of personal choices on the environment and communities is significant. By embracing sustainable fashion, individuals can reduce waste, conserve resources, and support ethical practices. These actions contribute to a greener and more ethical fashion industry, demonstrating the power of individual responsibility in promoting sustainability.

For those looking to embark on their own sustainable fashion journey, there are several tips and resources available. Researching ethical brands, learning about sustainable materials, and exploring upcycling and DIY projects can provide valuable insights and inspiration. Additionally, connecting with like-minded individuals and participating in community initiatives can offer support and encouragement.

Personal journeys in sustainable fashion highlight the importance of individual responsibility and the potential for positive change. By sharing their stories and experiences, individuals can inspire others to embrace sustainability and contribute to a more ethical and environmentally conscious fashion industry.

15

Chapter 15: A Call to Action

As we conclude "EcoThreads: Smart Fashion for a Sustainable Future," it is essential to reflect on the key takeaways and the importance of collective action in promoting sustainable fashion. The journey towards a greener and more ethical fashion industry requires the commitment and collaboration of designers, brands, consumers, and policymakers.

Throughout this book, we have explored the environmental and social impact of fast fashion, the principles of sustainable fashion, and the innovative materials and technologies driving the movement. We have also highlighted the role of consumers, ethical fashion brands, and traditional techniques in promoting sustainability. By understanding these elements, we can make informed choices and advocate for positive change.

The importance of collective action in promoting sustainable fashion cannot be overstated. By working together and supporting ethical practices, we can drive significant change within the industry. Brands can adopt sustainable materials and production methods, consumers can make conscious fashion choices, and policymakers can implement regulations to promote sustainability.

Inspiring stories of change and progress within the industry demonstrate the potential for positive impact. From visionary designers and innovative technologies to personal journeys and community initiatives, the sustainable fashion movement is gaining momentum. These stories serve as a reminder that every action counts and that we all have a role to play in creating a more sustainable future.

To conclude, here are some actionable steps individuals can take to promote sustainable fashion:

1. Educate yourself about the environmental and social impact of fashion.
2. Support ethical brands and prioritize quality over quantity.
3. Embrace second-hand shopping, upcycling, and clothing swaps.
4. Advocate for transparency and accountability within the fashion industry.
5. Participate in community initiatives and engage with sustainability-focused organizations.
6. Share your knowledge and experiences with others to raise awareness.

By taking these steps, we can contribute to a greener and more ethical fashion industry. The journey towards sustainable fashion is ongoing, and it requires the collective effort of all stakeholders. Together, we can create a positive and lasting impact on the planet and society.

Description: EcoThreads: Smart Fashion for a Sustainable Future

In a world where fast fashion dominates and environmental concerns are at an all-time high, "EcoThreads: Smart Fashion for a Sustainable Future" takes readers on an inspiring journey toward a more ethical and eco-friendly fashion industry. This captivating book follows the visionary path of Aisha Adeyemi, a talented fashion designer from Lagos, Nigeria, who dreams of revolutionizing fashion by merging traditional craftsmanship with cutting-edge technology.

From the bustling markets of Lagos to the prestigious fashion institutes of Paris, Aisha's story is one of passion, perseverance, and innovation. Alongside her tech-savvy partner, Lucas, Aisha embarks on a quest to create EcoThreads, a fashion brand that champions sustainable materials, fair-trade practices, and smart textiles. Their groundbreaking invention, EcoFiber—a fabric made from recycled plastic bottles—serves as a testament to their commitment to environmental responsibility.

CHAPTER 15: A CALL TO ACTION

Throughout the book, readers will explore the detrimental impact of fast fashion, discover the principles of sustainable fashion, and meet the pioneers who are driving positive change within the industry. With rich storytelling and real-life examples, "EcoThreads" delves into innovative materials, technologies, and the pivotal role of consumers in fostering sustainability.

The book also highlights the importance of traditional techniques, the power of ethical fashion brands, and the potential of a circular economy. By weaving together personal journeys and actionable insights, "EcoThreads" empowers readers to make informed choices and contribute to a greener, more ethical fashion future.

Whether you're a fashion enthusiast, an eco-conscious consumer, or simply curious about the future of fashion, "EcoThreads: Smart Fashion for a Sustainable Future" offers a compelling and hopeful vision for a world where style and sustainability go hand in hand.

www.ingramcontent.com/pod-product-compliance
Lightning Source LLC
LaVergne TN
LVHW020501080526
838202LV00057B/6096